T0012145

This Kid Has a Fish
The Short I Sound

By Connor Stratton

level
1
little blue
readers

www.littlebluehousebooks.com

Copyright © 2024 by Little Blue House, Mendota Heights, MN 55120. All rights reserved. No part of this book may be reproduced or utilized in any form or by any means without written permission from the publisher.

Little Blue House is distributed by North Star Editions:
sales@northstareditions.com | 888-417-0195

Produced for Little Blue House by Red Line Editorial.

Reading Consultant: Andrew P. Johnson, PhD, Distinguished Faculty Scholar and Professor of Literacy Instruction, Minnesota State University, Mankato

Photographs ©: iStockphoto, cover, 5 (fish), 5 (gift), 5 (hits), 5 (kicks), 5 (pig), 5 (sick), 5 (skips), 5 (stick), 5 (trip), 6, 9, 11, 13 (top), 13 (bottom), 19, 21, 23 (bottom); Shutterstock Images, 5 (kid), 5 (mitt), 5 (sit), 15, 17, 23 (top)

Library of Congress Control Number: 2023909727

ISBN
978-1-64619-924-2 (hardcover)
978-1-64619-942-6 (paperback)
978-1-64619-977-8 (ebook pdf)
978-1-64619-960-0 (hosted ebook)

Printed in the United States of America
Mankato, MN
102023

About the Author

Connor Stratton writes and edits nonfiction children's books. He lives in Minnesota.

Table of Contents

Consultant Note

"On It, Phonics!" is designed to reinforce vowel sounds, beginning blends, and sight words and to provide reading practice for young readers. Books like these are one important part of a comprehensive literacy program for students at emergent and beginning levels. "On It, Phonics!" should be used with other high-quality children's books. Instructors and parents are advised to go over the words in the picture glossary before students begin reading, and review the sight words after students finish reading. You can also ask students to go back and identify words with the target letter-sound.

Andrew P. Johnson, PhD,
Distinguished Faculty Scholar and
Professor of Literacy Instruction,
Minnesota State University, Mankato

Short I Picture Glossary

fish

gift

hits

kicks

kid

mitt

pig

sick

sit

skips

stick

trip

This Kid

This kid has a pig.

The pig is big.

This kid has a fish.

It is a little fish.

This kid has a stick.

This kid kicks.

This kid skips.

kicks

skips

13

These kids sit.

sit

This kid is on a trip.

This kid gives a gift.

This kid is sick.

sick

This kid has a mitt.

This kid gets a hit.

Sight Words

a	likes
big	little
gets	on
gives	the
has	these
is	this
it	to